TOOLS FOR TEACHERS

- **ATOS:** 0.9
- **GRL:** B
- **WORD COUNT:** 31

- **CURRICULUM CONNECTIONS:** nature, plants

Skills to Teach

- **HIGH-FREQUENCY WORDS:** be, can, have, make
- **CONTENT WORDS:** flowers, food, fruit, leaves, plants, roots, seeds
- **PUNCTUATION:** periods, exclamation point
- **WORD STUDY:** /oo/, spelled oo (*food*, *root*), ui (*fruit*); plural endings
- **TEXT TYPE:** information report

Before Reading Activities

- Read the title and give a simple statement of the main idea.
- Have students "walk" though the book and talk about what they see in the pictures.
- Introduce new vocabulary by having students predict the first letter and locate the word in the text.
- Discuss any unfamiliar concepts that are in the text.

After Reading Activities

Ask children to think of different kinds of plants they know of. Say their answers aloud, and encourage children to predict the first letter of each plant's name. Write their answers on the board and tally the number of children who are familiar with each kind of plant.

Tadpole Books are published by Jump!, 5357 Penn Avenue South, Minneapolis, MN 55419, www.jumplibrary.com

Copyright ©2018 Jump! International copyright reserved in all countries. No part of this book may be reproduced in any form without written permission from the publisher.

Editorial: Hundred Acre Words, LLC **Designer:** Anna Peterson

Photo Credits: iStock: Dole08, cover. Shutterstock: amenic181, 12–13; Billion Photos, 4–5; ER_09, 10–11; Jiratcha, 2–3; Juriah Mosin, 6–7; Madlen, 8–9; ZaZa Studio, 1. SuperStock: Jose Luis Pelaez/Blend Images, 14–15

Library of Congress Cataloging-in-Publication Data
Names: Mayerling, Tim, author.
Title: I see plants / by Tim Mayerling.
Description: Minneapolis, Minnesota: Jump!, Inc., 2017. | Series: Outdoor explorer | Audience: Age 3–6. | Includes index.
Identifiers: LCCN 2017045154 (print) | LCCN 2017044082 (ebook) | ISBN 9781624967207 (ebook) | ISBN 9781620319437 (hardcover: alk. paper) | ISBN 9781620319444 (paperback: alk. paper)
Subjects: LCSH: Plants—Juvenile literature.
Classification: LCC QK49 (print) | LCC QK49 .M39 2017 (ebook) | DDC 580—dc23
LC record available at https://lccn.loc.gov/2017045154

I SEE PLANTS

by Tim Mayerling

TABLE OF CONTENTS

tadpole books

I SEE PLANTS

leaf

**Plants can
have leaves.**

seed

Plants can have seeds.

flower

Plants can
have flowers.

fruit

Plants can have fruit.

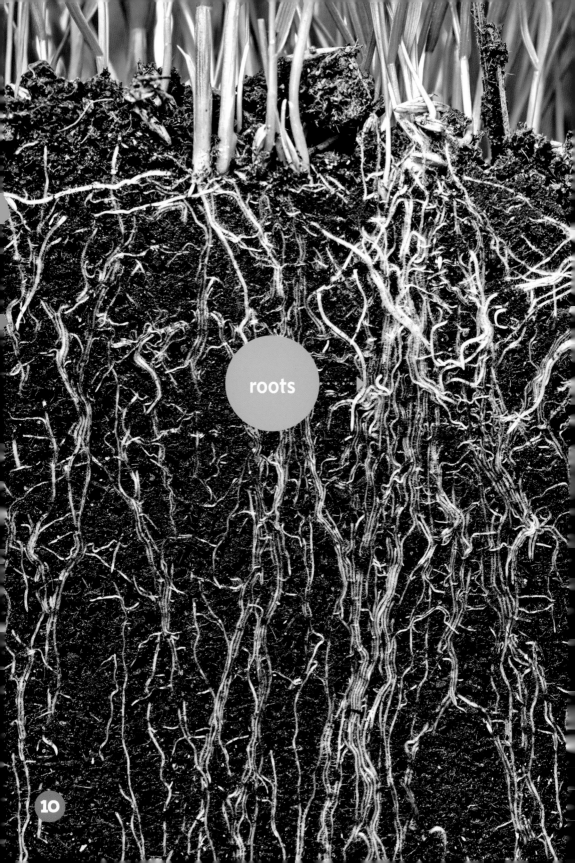

roots

Plants can have roots.

Plants can make food.

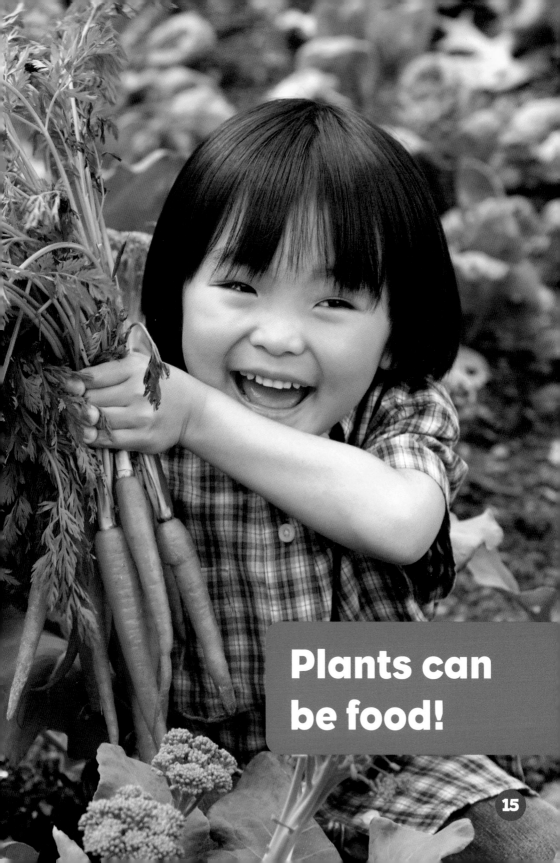

Plants can be food!

WORDS TO KNOW

flowers

food

fruit

leaves

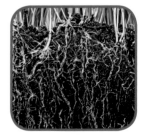
roots

seeds

INDEX